Budapest
Bend of the Danube

Budapest
Bend of the
Danube

Folpress Publishing, 2005

H U N G A R Y
Talent for entertaining

The author and the publisher express their gratitude to the
Hungarian Tourism Ltd. for their invaluable help.

Published by Folpress Publishing Company

Publishing Director: Imre Várlaki, director of Folpress Publishing Company

Editor: Éva Fizil

Editing Director: Mihály Gera

Design: Imre Horváth

Translator: Zsuzsanna Gaspar

Typography and printing: Folpress Printing Company

Photos: © Zoltán Gaál

Text: © András Székely

ISBN 963 86885 1 3

The Renaissance Italy, a millennium after the demise of the Roman Empire and five centuries before the birth of modern Italy consisted of the Papal state and four other principalities and city-states. In addition, it reigned over a large „cultural colony" north of the Alps: the state of Hungary of King Matthias encompassing a number of ancient Roman provinces (Pannonia, Dacia) and former territories of Germanic and Hun tribes. The capital of this country, in size equaling that of Italy today, was Buda, built south of the sharp bend of the Danube East of Vienna. Between the town of Esztergom at the bend and Buda lies Visegrad where the King and his Italian-born wife spent their blissful days until he decided to conquer Vienna following his expansionist ambitions.

The walled-in town of Buda on the top of the hills slowly merged with Pest spreading across the river. Some think the unification is not complete even today: a citizen of Buda differs from one from Pest as a Milanese might from one from Naples or someone from Munich from another from Hamburg. At the time of King Matthias it was held

that Venice is the most beautiful among littoral towns, Florence among towns on the plane and Buda is unrivalled among hill towns.

The picturesque, lively town of Buda was taken in 1541 by the Turks marching against Vienna – if only as a side escapade and only by trickery. Since then it has been under siege or bombed innumerable times, notably in 1686, 1849 and lastly, for six weeks during the bitter winter of 1944-45. The bombs of this last battle brought a number of Medieval ruins to the surface, allowing historians and archeologists a closer look. Changes in the social structure of the country permitted the former royal castle and governmental quarter to be renovated as the presidential palace and a cultural center, housing the national art gallery, library and museum; commanding a panorama over the Danube that became part of the UNESCO World Heritage List. Five hundred years ago one of the first printed "best-sellers" of the time, Hartmann Schedel's world chronicle, paid tribute to this very panorama by including an authentic block-print of the view. While most other cities were represented by an "artist's rendering," the image about

the East portion of Buda remains a trustworthy and rich historic source even today.

The unified city has been evolving since 1830. Each of its two dozen districts reveals areas of special character: university quarters, suburban areas, wooded scenic areas within the city limits, outdoor swimming pools and Turkish baths, tourist areas like the Castle and the Downtown shopping district; the Medieval core of both cities, the used books street of Museum Boulevard built on the ancient city wall, and streets where almost every building houses an antique shop. There are areas that abound in restaurants and cafés, places housing the traditional spring and fall book fairs, late-summer music parades, wine festivals. The Danube itself is the traditional place where the most prominent holiday, August 20, is celebrated each year: in remembrance of the foundation of the Hungarian State a millennium ago, on the name-day of St. Stephen, our founding king. Mind you, Catholics around the world celebrate Stephen's day four days earlier, but then again, Hungarians are not known for their punctuality.

For a king to be beatified in 1083 a few miracles were

called for – and legend has it the miracles were a few days late in the case of Stephen. But when they finally happened, nothing stood in the way of the beatification.

Anyway, the story of Hungary appears to be a string of miracles. The founder St. Stephen wanted to avoid having his country as the periphery of either the German or the Byzantine Empire – he decided to ask the Pope himself for recognizing his kingdom with the coronation symbols. And with success. When 240 years later the Mongols (Tatars) occupied and half ruined the country the supreme Khan died and his tribes returned to their homeland to elect his successor. After that they decided that China might be a better target than Vienna would have been, which gave Bela the Fourth, then king of Hungary, a chance to rebuild the country and erect the castle of Buda, among others, as well. When the Arpad dynasty of the founding fathers died out, the most progressive modern thinkers among the many relatives vying for the throne succeeded: two talented Anjou defining the fate of the 14th century, after that an Emperor-King from the Luxembourg

house, Sigismund. Their example – and of course that of the Medicis – determined the political and intellectual course King Matthias followed: a King with no royal blood but a true Renaissance self-made man.

A few decades after the death of Matthias the fate that had haunted St. Stephen came to pass: the country became the battleground between forces of the East and the West, stretching from the age of the Habsburgs and the Turks aiming for Vienna to the Cold War of the late 20th century. In between a few sober and balanced rulers or politicians could bring decades of peace giving enough relief to fund the aristocratic and civil establishments of Budapest and the larger cities: theaters, libraries, shops, hotels and the general infrastructure – though not in a way they would have under more peaceful circumstances. Let us mention the case of the bridges over the Danube as an example: after 1848 their number jumped from one to six, only to be destroyed by bombs in 1945, to withstand the six-week siege a few days longer. Budapest was a "fort" for Hitler – Vienna was not. Though he fiercely hated Vienna, he did not

defend it for more than a few days.

Contrary to the early saying, Budapest was not the "fort of Christianity" as much as a bridge between East and West, between Celtic and Scythian worlds, Pannonia and Hunnia, the German-Roman and the Byzantine empires, between the European center and the periphery. The most Western city of the East, and the most Eastern of the West.

The first permanent bridge was built by another Stephen, the Count Széchenyi – the aristocrat open to all innovation and the one to coin the name Budapest, working hard to modernize the country. His statue stands in front of the Hungarian Academy of Science which he helped found in 1825, following a family tradition: his father had founded the National Museum and established the Széchenyi Library based on his own collection in the early 19th century. Stephen Széchenyi wanted to develop a European-style transportation system, industry and agriculture before possibly seceding from the Austrian empire of which the Hungarian Kingdom had long been part, albeit with its own crown and laws. Opposing his vision stood the politician Lajos Kossuth who saw independence as paramount before embarking on any modernization. Both men were part of the government of the 1848 revolution (recognized by the Emperor). Kossuth died in exile, Széchenyi took his own life in a Viennese mad house.

After the country lost two thirds of its territory in the Trianon peace accord following the First World War and two unsuccessful revolutions, a third Stephen – Stephen Bethlen – of the Hungarian history tried turning the country toward the modern world and the liberal democracies of Europe. During the ten years marked by his leadership as prime minister the country started to slowly recover, only to join Germany after the 1929 recession on the losing side of WWII. Ironically, Stephen Bethlen, who protected his own governor, Miklós Horthy, from Hitler to the very end and who was wanted for the German concentration camps; in the end died in the Soviet Union. Perhaps of natural causes, we'll never know, but it is certain that the Hungarian communists returning from Moscow and serving Stalin feared his talents most.

The nearly 800 year old Bu-dapest of today is a product of many ages. Partly – as recalled by ruins and reconstructed from archeological remains – Medieval. Some houses date back to the 18th century, mainly to the era of Maria Theresa Empress and Hungarian Queen. Others recall the Reform years between 1825 and 1848, yet others the time of the Dualism from 1867 to 1918, when the Emperor of Austria ruled as Hungary's king as well. In theory the dual countries enjoyed the same status; in reality, much less so, with the minorities (Czechs, Slovaks, Romanians and Croats) barely supporting the "Danube" Monarchy. Today it might occur to us – late – that it was a small European Union, lasting only until 1918.

A few good years between the two world wars brought considerable development to Budapest. Many historicizing civil establishments and Art Deco buildings (whether residential, banking, or memorial) were created in the two decades preceding WWI – the Parliament, the Fishermen's Bastion, the neo-Baroque Royal Castle complex, to name a few. The synagogues of the Theresa-town of Pest date back to the same time. (This quarter is starting to return to life from its long decades of decay.) And finally the artifacts of the private developments, representing the architecture of the 21st century, have entered the context of the buildings in the city. Banks, shopping malls, markets pay tribute to the role of money and commodity in our society. New churches, theaters, schools and sports facilities are built and the residents of the city – though increasingly succumbing to the power of television as typical in any other city of the world – will follow their beliefs, both religious and cultural; will root for their sports team and will attend school to obtain a degree that will open the door for them to an international world. The opportunities for Hungary in the beginning of the 21st century have reached the level where they were a hundred years ago. And as you look around yourself on a balmy summer night you'll see this wonderful city returning to its glorious life: with friendly hospitality, rich variety, pleasant atmosphere where the young enjoy life and so do the elderly who love youth. Budapest entertains both its cosmopolitan residents and their guests – the tourists.

ANDRÁS SZÉKELY

From the displays of the **MILITARY MUSEUM:** *fancy Hungarian Hussar uniform*

MILITARY MUSEUM – *its building was built in the 19th century as army barracks*

HUNGARIAN STATE ARCHIVES – *its Neo-Roman building has been housing the collection in Buda since 1785 (Samu Pecz, 1923)*

MARIA MAGDALENE CHURCH – *a church of the citizens of Buda, built around 1250, largely destroyed in 1944*

COUNT ANDRÁS
old Buda City Hal

MEDIEVAL HOUSE
despite having been

HADIK *field marshal's equestrian statue stands in front of the*
(Sculptor: György Vastagh, 1937)

BAROQUE COLUMN WITH
MEMORIAL STATUES
on the Holy Trinity Square
erected in 1713 to
commemorate the passing
of the plague in 1691

n the South-west streets of the Castle District have maintained their character
rebuilt in the 18th century

FISHERMEN'S BASTION – *Neo-Roman lookout tower and promenade (Architect: Frigyes Schulek, 1895–1902)*

THE HUNGARIAN NATIONAL GALLERY *in the former royal castle with the statue of King Matthias (Hunyadi, the First) hunting (Alajos Stróbl, 1904–06)*

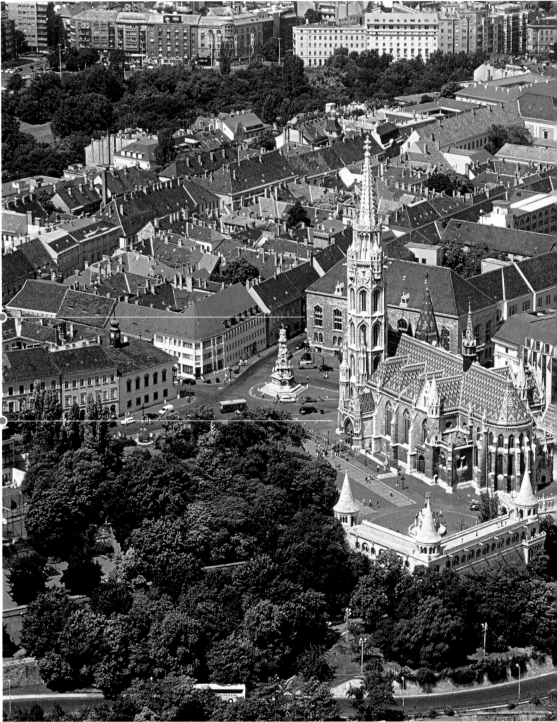

Bird's eye view of the **CASTLE HILL,** *from Southeast*

CHURCH OF THE VIRGIN MARY (MATTHIAS CHURCH) *originally from around 1245, reconstruction (1873–96) and altar by Frigyes Schulek, ornamental glass windows of the main altar designed by Károly Lotz and Bertalan Székely, depicting Hungarian saints*

ELISABETH, EMPRESS AND QUEEN – *bust in the Matthias Church*

The **NEO-BAROQUE ROYAL PALACE** – *West elevation with the 19th century Classicist Chain Bridge*

The **LIONS' GATE**
– *leading to the National Széchényi Library and the Budapest Historic Museum*

15TH CENTURY GOTHIC INTERIOR *reconstructed in the Buda Castle*

MEDIEVAL FOUNDATION WALLS – *frequent reconstructions and bombs of many wars left only this much of most buildings*

HUNGARIAN NATIONAL GALLERY
– *Pál Szinyei Merse: Lark, 1882*

WINGED ALTAR *in the Hungarian National Gallery – carved and painted Annunciation altar from around 1515*

PAINTED GOTHIC WOODEN STATUE
from the collection of the Matthias Church

STATUE FRAGMENT ADORNING A BUILDING
from the remains of Buda in the times of Sigismund

HUNGARIAN RANGE-MAN ON HIS HORSE
– *bronze statue by György Vastagh, around 1900, in front of the Hungarian National Gallery*

9TH CENTURY CLASSICIST TATUE *from the Castle District*

KING MATTHIAS – *hundred year old copy of a 15th century relief on the wall of the Hotel Hilton*

The **CITY'S GUARDIAN ANGEL PALLAS ATHENE** – *copy of the 18th century statue by Carlo Adami Italian master at the building of the old City Hall, facing the west elevation of the Matthias Church*

23

ARCHEOLOGICAL SITES

MAIN (DÍSZ) SQUARE

PALACE ALEXANDER

ARCHEOLOGICAL SITES IN THE CASTLE HILL – *facing is the President's Residence, next to the Castle Theater*

CASTLE THEATER – *German theater opened in 1787, where in 1790 a premiere was held in Hungarian*

HUNGARIAN NATIONAL GALLERY – *ornamental gate, with General Jenő Savoyai's statue beyond (József Róna, before 1900)*

The **FUNICULAR OF THE CASTLE HILL (1870)** –
*the destroyed and rebuilt cable-car offering splendid
views connects the Buda riverside with the Castle Hill*

The **0 KILOMETER MARK,** *on the Adam Clark
Square – statue by Miklós Borsos (1975)*

The **CHAIN BRIDGE AND THE TUNNEL** *(1849–56), with a square in betwee*

FRENCH INSTITUTE

TUNNEL

...med after Adam Clark, Scottish developer engineer, who became a citizen of Buda

HOUSE OF BENEDEK VIRÁG – *home of the 19th century poet historian. The memorial in front is by Pál Pátzay, from 1971*

The **GOLDEN DEER** – *residence rebuilt in 1811, the restaurant functioning inside is announced by the very sign-board of the original café*

MEDICAL MUSEUM – *including the entire interior of a pharmacy opened in 1813*

CASTLE GARDEN CASINO – *the elegant 19th century building contained the Royal Castle's waterworks' machinery; today it is a casino*

SAINT ANNE'S CHURCH on Batthyány Square (1724–1804); is held by many as the most beautiful Baroque church in Buda

The **MEMORIAL OF GÜL BABA** – Gül Baba, the dervish known for his love of roses, died in the year of Buda's siege by the Turks in 1541 – his funeral chapel built here is an Islamic place of pilgrimage

The **DUNA'S WATERFRONT IN BUDA** with the Saint Anne's Church and the Neo-Roman Lutheran church on the right
(Architect: Samu Pecz, 1893/96)

SHOPPING MALL MAMMUT

FÉNY U. MARKET

MOSCOW SQUARE – *the main traffic hub of Buda with the building of the Hungarian Post Office in the upper right*

*The **CITADEL** – the former fort with the Statue of Liberty, now without its original side figures depicting Soviet soldiers (Zsigmond*

(Kisfaludi Strobl, 1947)

GELLÉRT THERMAL BATH – *main entry*

GELLÉRT THERMAL BATH – *foyer*

The **GELLÉRT THERMAL BATH** (*Artur Sebestyén and others, 1912–18*

en-air pool

*The **MAIN SQUARE OF ÓBUDA** – from the entry of the Zichy Castle housing a number of museums dedicated to modern art*

The **SÍPOS** – *small restaurant known for its fish delicacies*

BAROQUE STATUE *on the Main Square of Óbuda*

◼ ANCIENT BUDA (ÓBUDA)

AQUINCUM
– *Jupiter the Roman God as manifested in a statue elevated on a column base in front of the museum*

AQUINCUM – *columns and foundation walls from Roman times*

AQUINCUM – *carved stone from the lapidarium (stone collection) of the museum*

AQUINCUM – *Roman family burial memorial*

ÓBUDA – *wall remnants of the colosseum serving the ancient Roman border guards*

PALATINUS OPEN-AIR SPA

SPORTS POOLS

HOTEL THERMAL

MARGARET BRIDGE

MARGARET ISLAND *and the base of the Castle Hill from Southwest*

MARGARET ISLAND – *The original Watertower; today an industrial memorial*

MARGARET ISLAND – *the main entry of the Grand Hotel at the North end of the Island*

ELISABETH BRIDGE

FREEDOM BRIDGE

LÁGYMÁNYOSI BRIDGE

The **BRIDGES OF BUDAPEST** *from the South: Lágymányosi, Petőfi, Szabadság (Freedom), Erzsébet (Elisabeth) and the Chain Bridge*

PETŐFI BRIDGE

SZABADSÁG (FREEDOM) BRIDGE

ONE OF THE FOUR STONE LIONS *guarding the Chain Bridge (János Marschalkó, 1852), with the Royal Castle in the background*

The **HUNGARIAN PARLIAMENT** *– Neo-Gothic building by Imre Steindl, 1884–1904*

The **PARLIAMENT** – *interiors with decorations conceived to illustrate the historical Hungary*

The **SAINT CROWN OF HUNGARY** *with the scepter and the orb – historical symbols of the monarchy respected by the republic as well*

The **DOME OF THE CUPOLA HALL**

The **SAINT STEPHEN BASILICA** (1851–1905) – the interior of the dome

The **CROSS OF CHRIST**
in the Basilica
(József Damkó, around
1900)

The **BASILICA** – the west façade with the main entrance

*The **BASILICA** – the main altar with the sculpture of King Saint Stephen – the revered relic, the King's right hand is also kept here*

The **HUNGARIAN NATIONAL BANK,** *originally the Austro-Hungarian Bank (Ignác Alpár, 1902–05)*

LEADED GLASS WINDOW *in the Hungarian National Bank (by Miksa Róth, around 1900 designe of most leaded glass windows and mosaics in the country)*

POST OFFICE SAVINGS BANK – *a prime example of the Hungarian A*

eco style (Ödön Lechner, 1900)

The **GRESHAM INSURANCE COMPANY** – *its palace originally high-end rental residences, today a five-star Four Seasons hotel*

The **HUNGARIAN ACADEMY OF SCIENCES** *(Architect: Friedrich August Stüler, 1865)*

rchitect: Zsigmond Quittner, 1907)

The **STATUE OF ISTVÁN SZÉCHENYI** *at the Academy (Sculptor: József Engel, 1880)*

The **DANUBE WATERFRONT IN PEST** – *its coherent view is on the UNESCO World Heritage List*

The **LITTLE PRINCESS** (*László Marton, 1990*)   **SUMMER OUTDOOR DINING** *on the Danube promenade*

*The **DANUBE PROMENADE** – spring, summer or fall, a popular breezy venue for strolls or people-watching*

ELISABETH SQUARE – *the Danubius Fountain (designed by Miklós Ybl, allegorical statues by Leó Feszler, 1880–83); on top the Danube as a male figure, below the Tisza and two smaller rivers of the country at the time represented by three female figures*

The **VIGADÓ CONCERT HALL** – *Eclectic building in a Hungarian Style (Architect: Frigyes Feszl, 1865) replacing the former Hall (Redout) destroyed by a bomb in 1849*

The **STATUE OF MIHÁLY VÖRÖSMARTY,** *poet (1800–55) on the square named after him, author of the Hungarian National Anthem (Sculptors: Ede Kallós and Ede Telcs, 1908)*

FERENC DEÁK SQUARE – *the traffic hub of Pest*

VÁCI STREET – *the avenue of fashion in Budapest*

The **UNIVERSITY LIBRARY** – *its reading room an exquisite remnant of past arts and sciences left behind from the 19th century*

CENTRAL CAFÉ – *recalling a civic lifestyle dominating the years between 1840 and 1940, but sill alive today*

RUDAS BATH

SERBIAN CHURCH IN PEST

LÓRÁND EÖTVÖS UNIVERSITY

ELISABETH BRIDGE – *the largest-span bridge of the early 20th century of Europe, named after Queen Elisabeth*

STATUE OF SAINT GELLÉRT

INNER CITY PARISH CHURCH

LAJOS KOSSUTH STREET

KÁROLYI PALACE

The **GRAND MARKET HALL** – *the largest market hall in Pest and Buda built after 1900*

The **GRAND MARKET HALL** *– a modern steel and glass building inside, it epitomized the welfare of all at the time*

BUDAPEST CORVINUS UNIVERSITY OF ECONOMICS, *– proud alma mater of numerous exceptional experts of the field – a few British lords and US professors, among others*

KÁLVIN SQUARE CHURCH – *around 1800 Calvinists could acquire property only outside the central areas of Pest*

ERVIN SZABÓ LIBRARY – *in the former palace the central unit of a public lending library was set up by liberal Free Masons*

KÁLMÁN MIKSZÁTH SQUARE – *the former Sacré Coeur convent is now occupied by the Piarist order devoted to teaching since 1717*

ÜLLŐI BOULEVARD

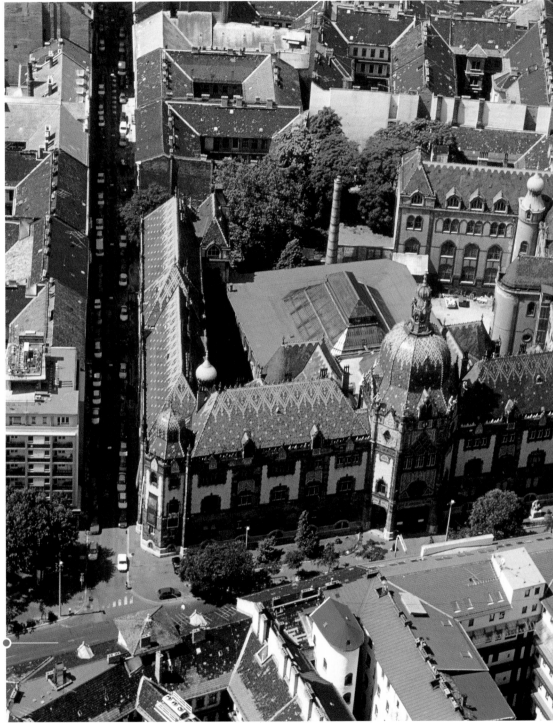

MUSEUM OF APPLIED ARTS – *the building opened for the Millennium of the State met with mixed public reception (Architec*

MUSEUM OF APPLIED ARTS – *an oriental example of the Secession style*

MUSEUM OF APPLIED ARTS – *an Eastern-European relative of Gaudí*

dön Lechner and Gyula Pártos, 1896)

NATIONAL MUSEUM – *façade (Architect: Mihály Polláck, 1846)*

NATIONAL MUSEUM
– *Quattrocento style Madonna*

NATIONAL MUSEUM
– *late Gothic church pew*

NATIONAL MUSEUM – *remnant of the time of King Lajos the 2nd*

NATIONAL MUSEUM – *duel armor from the early 16th century*

NATIONAL MUSEUM – *the head mask of King Saint László found in Győr, copy*

*The **GREAT SYNAGOGUE** (Architect: Ludwig Förster, 1859)*

The **INTERIOR OF THE GREAT SYNAGOGUE** – *a unique feature of the synagogue is the organ*

ANDRÁSSY BOULEVARD

OKTOGON – *initially named after Mussolini, later after the date of the Russian Revolution, November 7, the octagonal square* ▶

urned to its name recalling its shape

VÍGSZÍNHÁZ – *the elegant theater of the upper middle class in the district of ministries and banks (Architects: Ferdinánd Fellner and Hermann Helmer, 1896)*

VÍGSZÍNHÁZ – *detail of the 18th century style foyer*

NYUGATI (WEST) TRAIN STATION, *designed by the office of the French architect Gustave Eiffel (1877)*

The **NYUGATI (WEST) SQUARE** *changed names at least three times reflecting political changes*

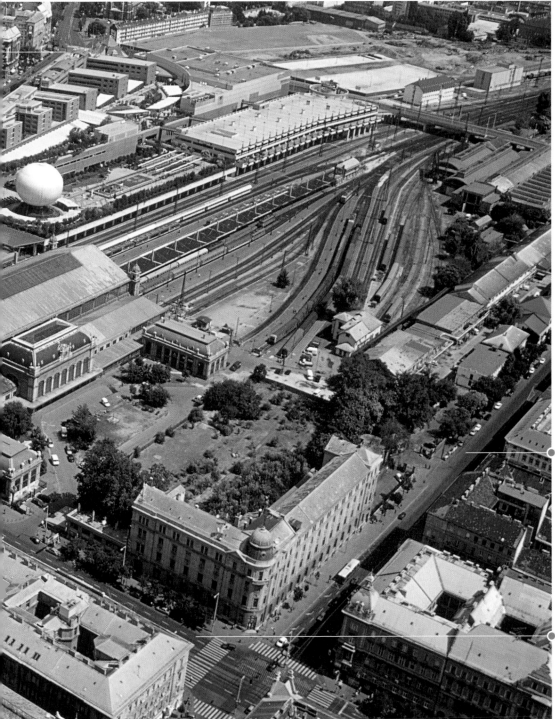

MUSIC ACADEMY
– *with leaded glass windows by Miksa Róth*

MUSIC ACADEMY
– *mosaic design by Aladár Körösfői Kriesch*

MUSIC ACADEMY – *the music hall (built in 1901–07) with outstanding acoustics and the organ*

MUSIC ACADEMY – *Eclectic façade (Architects: Flóris Korb and Kálmán Giergl) with the statue of Franz Liszt by Alajos Stróbl*

■ THERESA TOWN (TERÉZVÁROS)

CAPITAL OPERETTA THEATER – *once an elegant night club*

ANDRÁSSY BOULEVARD AND HEROES' SQUARE – *the historic figures*

MAI MANÓ HOUSE – *photographic art center in a former artist's loft*

ANDRÁSSY BOULEVARD – *under the wide and busy radial road runs Continent's first subway line*

the Square form the grand termination point of the boulevard

NDRÁSSY BOULEVARD – *shaded promenade*

ANDRÁSSY BOULEVARD – *outdoor café*

*The **HUNGARIAN STATE OPERA** – the elegant Neo-Renaissance façade (Architect: Miklós Ybl, 1875)*

The **HUNGARIAN STATE OPERA** – *auditorium*

KODÁLY KÖRÖND – *once the square housing the statues of nobility loyal to the Habsburgs, erected by Ferenc József the 1st*

The **OPERA HOUSE** *and its vicinity (the former Goethe Institute in the upper right hand corner now housed in Ráday stree*

ing the former Institute of Ballet being re-fitted as a hotel)

The **POST OFFICE MUSEUM** – *elegant interior from around 1880*   The **POST OFFICE MUSEUM** – *the dispatcher*

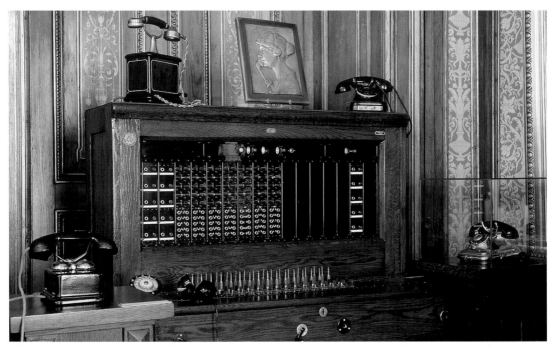

The **POST OFFICE MUSEUM** – *Tivadar Puskás, assistant to Edison, was a pioneer of the telephone switchboard*

HOPP FERENC MUSEUM – *a rich private collection of art from East and South Asia*

HEROES' SQUARE – *Millennium Monument, Museum of Fine Arts, Palace of Arts*

MŰCSARNOK

MŰCSARNOK (HALL OF ARTS) – FAÇADE *(Schikedanz and Herzog) with fresco painting by Jenő Medveczky and mosaic by*

GUNDEL RESTAURANT *next to the Zoo – centuries of Hungarian tradition, American–Hungarian management*

GUNDEL RESTAURANT *– Interior*

nő Haranghy

The ZOO – Main Entrance (Kornél Neuschloss, 1912)

The **ZOO** – *The elephant and hippopotamus house with eastern-style decoration*

The **AMUSEMENT PARK** – *Merry-go-round recalling the original fair*

SZÉCHENYI BATHS – *A thermal well yielding 77°C hot water, hidden in a Baroque castle from 1910: thermal and steam bath.*

d pools large enough to serve thousands

■ CITY PARK (VÁROSLIGET)

SZÉCHENYI BATHS – *ornamental façade*

SZÉCHENYI BATHS – *pools emitting steam worthy of a geyser*

SZÉCHENYI BATHS – *a popular pastime in the pool: chess*

VAJDAHUNYAD CASTLE

building complex museum from 1896 recalling glorious moments of the Hungarian History (by Ignác Alpár)

The **HUNGARIAN STATE INSTITUTE OF GEOLOGY** – *a unique Secession-style building by Ödön Lechner from the end of t*

9th century

The **NATIONAL THEATER** – *the Neo-Avantgard Eclecticism greets the 21st century (Architect: Mária Siklós)*

The **PALACE OF ARTS** – *redefining the spirit of the Concrete; from the studio of Gábor Zoboki*

The **PALACE OF ARTS** – *the entry stairs and colonnade of ageless elegance*

The **PALACE OF ARTS,** *housing among others the modern art exhibit of the Budapest Ludwig Collection*

The **NAGYTÉTÉNY CASTLE MUSEUM** – *Baroque-Rococo building from the 18th century...*

...housing the **FURNITURE COLLECTION OF THE MUSEUM OF APPLIED ARTS**

In the grand and intimate spaces of the museums the European and Hungarian artifacts from between 1450 and 1850 recall the quotidian details of the past

The **GÖDÖLLŐ CASTLE** – façade recalling the times of Maria Theresa Empress and Queen

The **GÖDÖLLŐ CASTLE**
– the marble bust of
Elisabeth Empress and
Queen

The **GÖDÖLLŐ CASTLE'S** theater of a past with vicissitudes is now
renovated to its former glory

*The **GÖDÖLLŐ CASTLE** – Queen Elisabeth's bronze statue in the castle park*

SZENTENDRE – *the cross of Orthodox Serbian tradesmen on the Main Square*

SZENTENDRE – *the museum of Margit Kovács, a ceramist working in the Art Deco style*

SZENTENDRE – *Rococo iconostas from the 18–19th century*

MARGIT KOVÁCS: *Boy with potter's wheel, 1929*

PRAVOSLAVIC MADONNA *in Szentendre's Blagovestenska church*

VISEGRÁD, CITADEL – *built by King Bela the 4th and his Byzantine wife after the times of Mongol attacks as a last place of refug*

VISEGRÁD – *residence of Medieval kings of Hungary*

VISEGRÁD – *Gothic fountain from the heyday of the castle*

VISEGRÁD – *ancient blocks of stone speak of the strength of the fort*

...and this reconstructed pool of the elegance of the 14–15th centuries

FERRY – *between Visegrád and Dömös*

ESZTERGOM – *the 18th century cathedral is the seat of the highest Catholic dignitary of Hungary*

ESZTERGOM – *inside the cathedral the reconstructed 16th century marble chapel of Tamás Bakócz archbishop, nominee for Pope, is a main attraction*

ESZTERGOM

ESZTERGOM – *the castle: its resilience under siege convinced the king of the importance of modern city planning*

the bridge built in 2002 to replace its predecessor demolished in WWII connects the city with Slovakia